BIOGRAPHY & BOOKS

BI⬚GRAPHY
& B⬚⬚KS

Edited by John Y. Cole
Executive Director, The Center for the Book

Library of Congress   *Washington 1986*

"The Question of Biography" copyright © 1986 by Samuel S. Vaughan
"The Art of Biography" copyright © 1986 by Edmund Morris
"George Washington in Print and on Television" copyright © 1986 by James
Thomas Flexner
"Biography in the City of Washington" copyright © 1986 by David McCullough

Library of Congress Cataloging-in-Publication Data
Main entry under title:

Biography & books.

    Papers originally presented at a symposium held Nov. 9–10, 1983 at the
Library of Congress and sponsored by the Center for the Book.
    Bibliography: p.
    1. Biography (as a literary form)—Congresses.
2. United States—Biography—Congresses.   I. Cole,
John Young, 1940–   .   II. Center for the Book.
III. Title: Biography and books.
CT21.B467   1986   808'.06692   85-600291
ISBN 0-8444-0520-5 (alk. paper)

∞ The paper used in this publication meets the requirements for
permanence established by the American National Standard for Information
Sciences "Permanence of Paper for Printed Library Materials," ANSI
Z39.48-1984.

CONTENTS

PREFACE

Why is biography so popular? Is biography an art? How does a biographer choose a subject? These were three of the questions discussed but of course never fully answered at a symposium about the writing, the publishing, and the influence of biography held at the Library of Congress on November 9 and 10, 1983. A celebration of books, the symposium was sponsored by the Center for the Book in the Library of Congress. More than thirty biographers (listed on p. 68) joined with publishers, editors, librarians, and readers to exchange ideas about the most popular form of nonfiction in the United States. Most of the biographers had used the Library of Congress in their research, and several were working full-time at the Library on new books at the time of the symposium.

Over 1,600 new books classed as "biography" were published in the United States in 1982, according the *The Bowker Annual*, and the number climbed to over 2,000 in 1983. In its 1978 and 1983 surveys of reading and book purchasing, the Book Industry Study Group found biography (including autobiography) to be the most widely read nonfiction category; in 1983, nearly four in ten book readers (38 percent) had read at least one biography in the previous six months. And biography continued its growth in popularity among book purchasers during 1984, according to a Gallup survey reported in the October 7, 1984, issue of *Publishers Weekly*.

The rapid success of *People* magazine, the fashionableness of personality columns, and the ubiquity of "personal profiles" are additional signs of increased interest in "other people's lives." The trend is also evident in universities and in libraries. Biographical research centers have been established at the University of Hawaii (which publishes the quarterly journal *Biography*) and at Griffith University in Brisbane, Australia.

Genealogical research is more popular than ever. Noting "an apparently unquenchable thirst" for biographical information, a committee of the American Library Association in 1982 began a survey of biographical reference sources. The listing was limited to English-language books currently available from U.S. publishers or distributors and excluded genealogical sources, works primarily of local interest, and so-called "vanity" works. In spite of these exclusions, the compilers still found enough reference works "to bewilder and amaze both library users and librarians." Over 190 biographical sources are listed in the May and June 1984 issues of the Association's *Booklist*, ranging alphabetically from *The Academic Who's Who* to *The Writer's Directory*, and many are multivolume sets.

Biography is a natural subject for exploration by the Center for the Book in the Library of Congress. Established by law in 1977 to stimulate public interest in books, reading, and the printed word, the Center for the Book brings together members of the book, educational, and business communities for projects and events that enhance the role of books in our society. It is financed primarily by private contributions from corporations and individuals. The center is grateful to the following for their support of the biography symposium: Gale Research Company, Marquis Who's Who, CBS Television, Encyclopaedia Britannica, and Clare Boothe Luce. Thanks also go to the four principal speakers whose remarks are published in this volume: publisher Samuel S. Vaughan, biographer Edmund Morris, historian James T. Flexner, and writer and biographer David McCullough. Their contributions and those of the other biographers, editors, and publishers present made the occasion a memorable one for all who are interested in "telling lives."

John Y. Cole
Executive Director
The Center for the Book

The Symposium

November 9 and 10, 1983

Welcome

Daniel J. Boorstin

⊞ Welcome to the Library of Congress. We are indebted to all of you—biographers, publishers, critics, readers—for joining us here. We are grateful to you for enriching our American literature, and we hope this occasion will remind you of what we at the Library of Congress can or should do to help you in your future work. Your invitation here is an accolade and a thanks to you for the part you have played in teaching us and entertaining us with American lives and lives of the world's heroes. We also thank you for helping us make this great library a forum of our culture and a forum for those who have helped enrich it.

It is appropriate that we should have chosen biography as our genre. Biography is a literary form in which Americans have been peculiarly successful and versatile, and which has especially appealed to American readers and book-buyers. Also, of course, this genre has an intimate and vivid relation to history, to the resources and the making of the Library of Congress. Our three buildings—named after Thomas Jefferson, John Adams, and James Madison—commemorate figures who have invited some of the best talents of American biographers. Our manuscript collection is largely a collection of biographic sources. Here on Capitol Hill, of all places, we are at a point of intersection of individual and collective biography, of the characters, hopes, ambitions, and frustrations of individual men and women, and the vectors of social purpose.

In talking about biography, it is hard not to be sententious. Reckless and dogmatic pundits, at least since Emerson and

11

Carlyle, have quipped that all history is biography or that all biography is history. Today, with the help of our best practitioners of biography we hope to transcend such banalities. Speaking as an aficionado of biography, but emphatically not as a biographer, I find biography the most enticing and irresistible form of history. Perhaps because it is for me the most meandering form, and I enjoy the meanders. For me the secrets of biography are the most tantalizing, and its revelations are the most puzzling. We will explore together some of these secrets and revelations.

We cannot avoid asking, What is the proper territory of the biographer? Or is this a proper question? A talented biographer, Philip Guedalla, said that biography is a region bounded on the north by history, on the south by fiction, on the east by obituary, and on the west by tedium.

We may also ask, What is the proper character of a biographer? And we may be chastened by Oscar Wilde's question. Why is it, he asked, that every great man nowadays has his disciples, and why is it always Judas who writes the biography? But would we really be better off if the biography were written by a Saint Paul or a Saint Peter?

We look forward to an illuminating two days of conversation and exploration.

The Question of Biography

Samuel S. Vaughan

We are here to celebrate biography, but I think at the same time we ought to try to advance the understanding of biography. For when we speak of celebrating biography, we speak of celebrating life, or lives. We are speaking of nothing less than saving lives or raising them, most often from the dead. In Washington, D.C., where it seems so difficult to advance the art of the state, perhaps we can help advance the state of the art.

Let us celebrate later, nearer the end, where celebrations belong. First, there are a couple of questions I would like to put in the air. One of the easy aspects of being an editor, rather than a professor, is that you get to ask questions to which you do not have the answers. Some are obvious, such as, "What is biography?" The companion question, of course, is that ceaselessly interesting and galling one, "What is history?" Those questions are eternal, and I hope that my speech and your answers will not be as long.

We know Henry Ford's famous four-letter definition of history, but "bunk" doesn't quite do it. Thomas Carlyle said that history is nothing more than the biography of great men, which is probably why you hear so little about Carlyle from great women. We also know his remark that "a well-written life is almost as rare as a well-spent one." But I did not know, until I read the book *Telling Lives,** which some of the people in this audience created, about Jane Carlyle, who once

---

Telling Lives: The Biographer's Art, ed. by Marc Pachter. Philadelphia: University of Pennsylvania Press, 1981.

13

responded to a less-than-honest letter from her husband by saying, "That letter will read charmingly in your biography."

As explained in Daniel Boorstin's stunning book *The Discoverers*, Carlyle had a predecessor, one of the great Muslim historians of India writing in the mid-fourteenth century. "History," this scholar said, "is the knowledge of the annals and traditions of prophets, caliphs, sultans, and of the great men of religion and government. . . . Low fellows, rascals, unfit people of unknown stock and mean natures, of no lineage and low lineage, loiterers and bazaar loafers—all these have no connection with history." I think his was a wonderful injunction. Of course, if we followed it today, it would put biographers, publishers, and other low fellows out of business.

Still there are those who would say that only great people are worthy of biography. Just as there are those who claim that tragedy can only befall the high and the mighty, that the only suitable subjects for biography are Montaigne and Metternich and Churchill, not Charlie Parker or Jackie Robinson or Marilyn Monroe. Of course, in a messily democratic society, we very often confuse the great with the merely notorious, the truly distinguished with those who are truly well known. Dr. Boorstin has pointed out elsewhere that some of us are well known for our well-knownness, rather than for our accomplishments.

Edmund Gosse said that "biography is the faithful portrait of a soul in its adventures through life," which I find a terrifying description. Elizabeth Hardwick, on the other hand, said that "biographers are the quick in pursuit of the dead." Robert Gittings sees biography as closer to poetry than other forms, while Michael Holroyd sees it as more like the novel and Ronald Clarke finds it cousin to history. Asked recently if biography is a hybrid, Gittings said, "I believe in Desmond McCarthy's dictum that the biographer is an artist. But an artist on oath."

It is quite possible that these questions, of biography and of history, are a nagging part of that larger backache, "What is life?" or, worse, "What is truth?" Librarians—and I speak with affection of those in whose house we meet—classify biography with autobiography and memoirs. I think of each of those as being quite different. Although obviously related, they are really, each to the other, poor relations.

Sadly, I do not think that in the next two days we will be able to consider at any length the memoir, which is neither well-practiced nor well-understood in this country. We have seen the decision of modern presidents to tell all, or at least to tell a little at great length, usually in several volumes. This recall tradition also extends to secretaries of state as well as secretaries of other kinds. Last month I was approached by a man who wanted me to pursue the journal, or the memoir, of one of Hitler's secretaries, who is said to be alive and well. On asking John Toland, Hitler's biographer, I learned that most of Hitler's secretaries are alive and well, and most think their boss has been misunderstood. All of which would have quenched my desire for a Hitler's secretary book, if I had had one in the first place.

We all know the American tendency in biography, which is something like the California strawberry: too big, too lacking in flavor, and shaped only approximately the right way. Americans tend to produce biographies as we once produced automobiles, fat with features and spendthrift of energy. Yes, this is a very American tendency. You remember who said the following: "The art of biography seems to have fallen on evil times . . . those two fat volumes, with which it is our custom to commemorate the dead, who does not know them, with their ill-digested masses of materials, their slipshod style, their tone of tedious panegyric, their lamentable lack of selection, of detachment, of design?" It was of course our patron saint, Lytton Strachey, in 1918. To which, wickedly, Joseph Epstein added more recently: "That description, two volumes and all, fits nothing so well as Michael Holroyd's *Lytton Strachey*, which appeared fifty years later." *Question:* why, the bigger biographies become, the more do they seem to diminish their subjects?

Recently John Russell, reviewing a biography of Baron James Rothschild by Anka Muhlstein, said that everything about the story was outsize except the book itself. Muhlstein, he said, is "that rare thing in the 1980's, the biographer who travels light." Her new book "ranges the length and breadth of Europe, has to do with the waxing and waning of vast fortunes, the making and breaking of kings and queens and governments, and the evolution of distinctive 'Rothschild Taste' . . . yet it goes barely above two hundred pages."

All of which reminds me somehow of a comment by a contemporary Rothschild, who was asked not long ago by an interviewer to what he attributed his family's centuries-long ability to both conserve and increase their capital. "My family," he said, "has always been known for taking its profits too early." Perhaps there is a lesson there too for biographers and their editors.

I have been asked to speak about biography partly from the perspective of a working editor and publisher. A number of us in the room are flattered by the suggestion that publishers have any perspective at all. As an editor, I have had far more experience with autobiography than with biography, but any editor who really loves the business, loves the form; loves the learning as you go, loves biography as literature, which it occasionally becomes. Perhaps it would be helpful if I described two or three of my experiences with the publishing of biography.

In one instance—and I cannot use names here—the biographer chose his subject and we chose the biographer—but most of all the subject had chosen his biographer. They knew each other. They had worked together for years. They were, quite simply, made for each other. The subject was an interesting, complex political figure who came to national prominence in the 1950s and stayed there for decades. The author was a superbly equipped journalist, who had worked, as I say, for and with the subject and had mixed feelings of admiration and love and despair about him. Typically, the book was to take two or three years. Typically, it took ten. The writer produced a first draft of three million words.

With some reaction from my senior editorial associate, Ken

McCormick, and myself, mostly violent, he reduced that draft by almost a half, and with some work on our part, we reduced it further. But, of course, it took two volumes, published over the course of three or four years. The book, in one sense, had everything. It was a meticulous, scrupulous record of what the subject said and did, where he went and with whom. It had the author's view of the subject, for some reason mostly melancholy. As a source book, it was, and remains, magnificent. We had the author and the subject, both good. The only problem is we didn't have the biographer or a biography.

Let us turn to a case where we can name names. In the middle 1960s, our editor in Paris, Beverly Gordey, sent in reports on a biography by Henri Troyat of Leo Tolstoy. We responded with enthusiasm, but others had already said it for us. André Maurois's comment was, "I had wanted to write his biography myself. Troyat has written exactly what I would have liked to write."

Our own first reader's report was not bad, either. Ann Hemenway wrote, "You can get the story of Leo Tolstoy's life in a couple of thousand words in a reference book. What you will not get is the scent, the scene, the color of Russia in the middle of the nineteenth century—a society, by the way, which must have resembled the pre-Civil War American South to an extent that would astonish most Americans. You will not get such insights as," and then she quoted from the text, " 'There was nothing incongruous to this man that, on one day, he could write in his journal, "Slavery is an abomination," and on the next write to his brother, asking him to sell thirty-three serfs in order to pay his gambling debts.' "

One of the questions that we, as editors, ask about biography is, "What was the life?" This is not the same as "Was he important?" or "Did she do things?" What was the *life*? What were the events? What is the juice of the story? What were the contradictions of character? What was done and what was left undone; what is known, what unknown? You have got a subject; where is the *story*?

If the life was "merely" important but uneventful—and

that is often the case in the lives of writers, for example—then the subject is less promising as commerce and requires more art as biography. Leo Tolstoy led a *life*. He lived a long time, as you know. He was a soldier. He was an egotist. He was a writer as great as he thought he was, and he was a pamphleteer-educator not nearly as great as he thought he was. He was a man celebrated in his own time, a man exiled, a man restored. He was a man who loved his wife, a woman who, it was said, loved, in turn, nothing more than patiently copying and recopying the manuscripts that he handed out to her, impossibly scrawled, yard by yard, by the mile, over the years. Sonya Tolstoy may have been the first word processor.

From Troyat's biography, listen to Leo in defeat. "I was very pleased to learn that the Nobel Prize was not given to me. Firstly, because it spared me the great problem of how to dispose of the money, which, like all money, can only lead to evil. . . . And secondly, because it had given me the honor and pleasure of receiving such expressions of sympathy from so many highly esteemed although unknown persons."

He was, of course, also a romantic and a lover. He chased his wife around the bed until they were both deep into their eighties or deep into bed, and yet that woman had to sit in a railroad car on a siding, estranged, while he died slowly and painfully in the trainshed.

I will never forget the scene in the book in which young Leo Tolstoy is tapped for the privilege of going up to the bedroom with his grandmother. His grandmother would take one of the children to her chambers each night, where they would perform their ablutions, and she would settle down in her great big bed in a cloud of white, and he would settle down in a smaller trundle bed, and then the blind serf seated at the window would begin to tell his tale in a drawling voice. "Once there was a powerful king who had an only son . . . ." A terrific scene, a lovely scene, because you can feel here, in Troyat's description, the birth of a storyteller. Tolstoy's final service to literature was his life.

A few observations about one or two recurring biographical subjects. In the early 1960s, I was assigned by Ken McCormick to work on the Eisenhower memoirs just as John Kennedy's star had risen above the White House. I came to the Eisenhower assignment in the moment of one of Eisenhower's few defeats. To be sure, he could not have run for office again and would not have. But the candidate he wanted most had not been nominated, and the Republican nominee had not been elected. He felt that this was a setback.

We had sent Eisenhower out of office approximately as we had President Truman and as we would Presidents Johnson, Nixon, Ford, and Carter—disheveled and discredited. Those who are not carried out tend to be thrown out. God help our ex-presidents, for they need the help of history and suitable biographers.

Anyhow, with the indignities heaped upon President Eisenhower by the campaign—let us go forward, let us get the nation moving again, let us get out of this stagnation—sentiments I shared, by the way, for I had voted for John Kennedy and loved him—I went to work in Gettysburg. There, I began to learn the obvious: that there are not two sides to every story but an incalculable number of sides. Then we came to the awful start of the long season of assassinations, and, soon thereafter, fresh from the outrage of the killing of John Kennedy, came the outrageous, to me, hagiographic books. Like millions of other Americans, I admired Kennedy and the family in the White House, but I was increasingly agitated by the spate of books, most of which had about as much claim to durability or credibility as plastic campaign buttons or other souvenirs.

As the books spilled from the pens and presses, I drafted an article, "The Second Killing of Kennedy." The vast overestimation of John Kennedy's administration, of his contributions, of his decisions—these would, I believed, eventually help diminish him historically. Nobody would buy the article. It was not very good and the time was not right. But those books, some written out of pain, sorrow, or loss; some out of mimicry or opportunism or to gild by association, did their damage. What we are treated to now is a recession in the fortunes of John Kennedy historically. No matter. History and future biographers will have their way.

My upset, of course, took place while I was working with a team that was concerned with the historical reputation of Dwight D. Eisenhower. He was well-known then—a political general, a chairman of the board, a bit of a bumbler, genial, ineffectual, didn't know what was going on in his administration, and so on. It was said that it had been run by John Foster Dulles, or, alternatively, Sherman Adams or Milton Eisenhower or whomever—just a bunch of businessmen, bridge players, golfers, fools. At one point, while President Kennedy was still alive, the Organization of American Historians polled itself. Its members ranked American presidents, and they put Eisenhower very close to the bottom. When we were working on *Waging Peace*, the second volume, we said to him, "How do you think you're going to rank in history?" and he said, approximately, "It doesn't depend so much on what we did. It depends on the people who come after us. If they do well, then we'll look worse, and if they do worse, then we'll look better." Such insight appeared in print, but characteristically muted, and surrounded with more prose than it needed.

Well, you have seen what has happened. The revisionism of Eisenhower is an academic industry. Such revisions did not begin with his friends or apologists or defenders. It began with his adversaries, or, more importantly, with a handful of independent minds. Much of it began, to be specific, with Murray Kempton.

Kempton wrote a column years ago in which he described Eisenhower as a bit of a fox, as a far more subtle and far more effective man than we had realized. This was followed by other good and somewhat lengthier appraisals, those of Gary Wills, for example. And by now it is a major occupation. Prof. Fred Greenstein of Princeton is the latest to publish a reestimation of Mr. Eisenhower, another author coming from the liberal left, who sees now that in previous estimates his critics (as biographers sometimes do) missed the man.

Arthur Schlesinger, Jr., on leaving his work in the White House, remarked that as a historian, he would never again believe what he read in the newspapers. Which raises a question about historians who do, and which leaves us with a problem and a *Question*. If you cannot trust historians at least when polled on presidents, and you cannot trust journalists, whom can you trust?

At Doubleday, we like to publish biography and autobiography. Currently, we have 161 such books in print. They include James Flexner's lovely book on America's old masters, for instance, and a biography of B. B. King, blues singer. We have the indefatigable Asimov on science and technology, or on scientists and technologists, and a book on the Astor family, as well as one on John and Yoko, another on Justices Brandeis and Frankfurter, one on Ray Charles, and one on Charles Boyer. *The Confessions of St. Augustine* and *The Confessions of Gary Wills*, both seen as ex-conservatives, are on our list. We have a book on Diana, Princess of Wales, one on Elinor Wylie, one on Frederick Remington, and a book on the great violinists.

The autobiographies or memoirs tend to outnumber the biographies, but we pursue biography no matter what. We have in process the multiple-volume autobiography of Isaac Bashevis Singer. Of course, we have Irving Stone's *Jack London, Sailor on Horseback*, on a list that includes figures from Jane Fonda to Khruschev. My list of examples ends with that adventure in biography and autobiography and imagination by Alex Haley called *Roots*, and it begins, alphabetically almost (and as my own publishing career began), with the brief, neverending life described by Anne Frank.

How do they sell? Recently, we published a splendid biography of Cervantes, by William Byron, sales 4,000; an unexpected and acclaimed critical biography of Scott Fitzgerald by the French scholar André Le Vot, sales, so far, 6,000; a good biography of Albert Camus, by Herbert Lottman, sales about 11,000. And a book about Bruce Springsteen by Dave Marsh, sales of 104,000. You may find that appalling. I find it cheerful. At least some young people are reading as well as watching or listening. They want to know about their heroes and heroines, and not just heartbreak and heroin. One well-regarded biographer of Horowitz is now contemplating a biographical work with Michael Jackson. If you don't know who Michael Jackson is—and I didn't, I had to be briefed—there are people who don't know who Horowitz is. Remember this: Jackson is younger. He is twenty-four.

This is true of other generations. We have to face the fact that some people would rather be Frank Sinatra than vice president, and perhaps they are not wrong. At least as Sinatra, you would have some influence in government.

I am pleased that we have present here people who are doing biographical work with film and tape. My pre-publishing experience with biography was almost entirely at the hands of biographers who signed themselves Selznick or Mayer or roared their work, and, in some respects, I guess they were laughable, but, in other ways, laudable because they led me to the music, to Chopin and Gershwin, Cornell Wilde, Robert Alda, and all. Playwrights and moviemakers often choose the moment to represent the person, the turning point or the odd hour to illuminate the whole life. *Sunrise at Campobello*, for example, could be a lesson for those afflicted with biographical elephantiasis.

We do traditional biography, commissioned biography, decommissioned biography, authorized biography, protested biography, biographies of political figures and politicized biographies of political figures. To these categories, we might add a few others—the perfunctory biography, for example, which I think of as hack-iography, although that could easily be confused with biographies written axe in hand. Here is a proposal we entertained this week at a meeting. It is to be a biography of a recent president. The author-to-be, a well-known author and journalist, said "I could not write this biography with much objectivity, but I think I could maintain the guise of objectivity. The three chief malformities of his career should not be overdone. Only fellows like Victor Lasky have never learned that no matter how we Americans feel about our political cripples, we don't like for wise guys to kick them around unmercifully. When our tale is over, we do *not* want to have been so harsh that the reader sympathizes with the subject."

And that author is not alone. The writer Leon Harris, author of *Merchant Princes*, was asked whether the stories in his book are true.* He says, "Throughout this book I have been much more interested in the revealing and probable anecdote than in tiresome facts of unquestionable accuracy. I willingly confess my feeling, as expressed by the Abbé Raynal about Benjamin Franklin, that he would rather recount some men's stories than other men's truths."

I was invited here to raise questions, so let me raise a few. *Question:* Whatever happened to the regard for facts? Whoever allowed Norman Mailer to invent "factoids"? Or are they something that can be cleared up by nightly applications of ointment? *Question:* Would modern biography be better with more reliable fact-searching and, at the same time, fewer facts? *Question:* What are we to make of the claims for "psycho-biography"? Given the well-advertised shortcomings of professional psychiatry, what do we make of the biographer as amateur analyst? Presumably, no first-rate biography can be written without intelligent speculation into the manners and motives of the subject. Just as clearly, a great deal of bilge can be expelled by a biographer who decides to play not only God, but Freud. Can any biographer hope to escape the psychoanalyst's role? Should any biographer be allowed to diagnose, and perhaps prescribe, without a license?

Question: Is it helpful to know the subject? George Painter said recently, "I wouldn't have liked to have met any of my subjects. If somebody said, 'Proust called this evening, do look in and meet him,' I wouldn't have wanted to. I wouldn't have turned my head to see him across the street. The Proust I am interested in is the Proust living inside Proust's eyes, ears, and mouth. That's where I want to be. . . . "

---

*Leon A. Harris, *Merchant Princes: An Intimate History of Jewish Families Who Built Great Department Stores* (New York: Harper & Row, 1979).

Question: Should a biographer spend a lifetime on a life or half a lifetime on one or two lives?

Question: What are the rights of the biographer? Once, an author was bound by tradition and sometimes bound in chains if the authorities gave his book a bad review. Then, in this country, judicial and journalistic interpretation of the First Amendment opened things up, at least on any of us considered to be public figures. Almost anything goes . . . until lately, when certain decisions seem to be turning against the author and the publisher. The threat has been lessened somewhat by the decision of some publishers to take out insurance, not on the lives of authors but on their libel liabilities.

Question: What are the rights of the subject? What are the rights of the dead? What rights should survivors have? How comfortable are we with the licenses, literary and legal, on so-called public figures, and do their wives and children have any rights? Where do rights begin and end, and where do responsibilities begin, and should they ever end? *Question:* Whatever happened to taste?

Is there not some reason to suspect that, in some quarters, we are utterly losing our grip on what biography is or can be? I wonder whether the virtues and deficiencies of "investigative journalism" are being carried over into biography and whether one is being confused with the other. Are we mistaking an author's interviews for an author's intelligence? Are we cloudy about independence versus responsibility, conscientiousness versus conscience? As Edward R. Murrow said, in a certain connection, there is a fine line between investigation and persecution. He was speaking of—and I think to—Sen. Joseph McCarthy.

W. A. Swanberg wrote to Daniel J. Boorstin in a letter before this conference, "I found it difficult to make judgments of a subject's shortcomings. To attempt Christlike understanding can be boring and evasive, but one must not carp, and simple fairness seemed the best course." (See p. 63)

I am coming to realize that my problem and my questions center on the idea that when somebody says "biography," I think of a book of a certain quality, even though I suppose the word simply suggests a book about a life, not necessarily a good book about a life. The word stands for a category, not an accomplishment. Still, it distresses me that hackwork as well as masterwork is called biography. Is biography well-received and well-understood in our country? Leon Edel remarks, in his letter about this conference, "I think the depth and extent of the biographical subject has scarcely been touched. And reviewers are lamentable: they review the subject but not the treatment." Mr. Edel's comment may be too sweeping, but he catches a good many people in his dustpan. Geoffrey Wolff, meanwhile, endures criticism about his choice of subjects for being what is called "minor."

Perhaps the last *Question* should be, Is biography impossible? Perhaps biography is one of the tragic arts, like the translation of poetry or writing about music, doomed from the start. The great poem, written in its own language, is inherently untranslatable. Music cannot be heard on the page, at least by nonmusicians. And maybe the great life fully lived is not susceptible to full resurrection. Think of the impossibility of capturing a life on paper, in one or two or twenty volumes. Think of the impossibility of capturing this moment, in this room. Here, in these seats, one of you is indigestive; another is indecisive, wondering whether to leave. Three of you have headaches. Six others have better questions than mine. Some are here to talk about biography, and some of you are here for other reasons. To some, the setting is wonderful—a national treasure. To others, it is American marbleized overstatement at its most grandiose. Thirty-two of you are listening to what I am saying, after a fashion, and at least a dozen wish they were back in bed. Think of this moment and the impossibility of capturing it. Does that make the writing of history and biography impossible or just difficult and brave?

And one more. Here in this town, where so many lives are led, to which so many people are led, biographies are being lived out in their first, rough-draft form, the version called life. Mr. Reagan, a number of the people in this room, and a number of people within ten blocks of here will have their lives told by others. *Question:* Are they living them in the consciousness that this will happen? How strong is their sense of history, of biographical destiny? We are told that the examined object changes by the very fact of examination, but does the object change *before* it is examined, in anticipation of examination? What documents are created to affect that inevitable examination, to read "charmingly" in the memoirs and biographies to come? And to what extent is this good— or otherwise?

Perhaps no recent president tried more consciously and obviously to manipulate his biographers than Lyndon Johnson. He did everything from court them to provoke them, from withholding information to supplying it in quantity, and especially to underscoring, with a long jab of a long finger, the points that he thought ought to be made. He did it with Doris Kearns and with Bill Moyers and with Harry McPherson and with visiting editors and with God knows, or Lyndon only knows, how many others. Mr. Nixon, meanwhile, understanding that he cannot rely on the kindness of strangers, is filling the air with books as did Herbert Hoover. He will try to have his way with history as he did with the presidency.

It has been said there are no definitive biographies, only versions of fiction. Naomi Bliven, reviewing Braudel,* remarks that his "absorbing and imposing volumes leave us awed at the work he has accomplished and also at the work that needs to be done before we begin to understand the past." It is a sobering thought that we have all those miles to go before we can even begin to understand and that, in troubled passage, we must go on trying to understand the past, including our own. Perhaps the combination of trying to understand the past and trying to understand ourselves is too much to contemplate, but the nice thing is that this is why we are here—and that is what you do, those of you who are biographers. Impossible or not, you bring it off. The best biographers bring them back alive. You stir the draperies, open

---

*Fernand Braudel, *Civilization and Capitalism, 15th–18th Century,* tr. Sian Reynolds, 3 vols. (New York: Harper & Row, 1982–83).

the drawers, let us feel the fire, smell the smoke, listen to the sound of another breathing in the room.

To do it, you need energy, ego, and humility in the face of facts and courage to face the cloud of unknowing. Oh, yes, you do need courage. When George Painter was asked about it recently, he said, "Courage is something I respect in others and have all too little of myself. I don't think I'm an optimist—I think this world is a terrible place, but I think that the work of the artists, and particularly the great writers, is the greatest thing that has happened in human life. Human life is what matters, and in these books, in these works of literary art, human life is being expressed at a deeper, more intense, more clear-sighted level than anything we can achieve ourselves. That's why we write biographies, and that's why we read them."

And thank you for doing them.

The Art of Biography

Edmund Morris

⎕ "Book persons"—to use a phrase indulged with complacency by those who are manifestly not—still cling to the delusion that fiction and poetry are the only creative forms of literature. Book persons resent the applications of the word *art* to biography. They point out that most biographies are trivial at best, and unnecessary at worst.

By the same token, we biographers are gossips or bores. We are indefatigable in researching the mating habits of Britain's royal family, and in telling the world rather more than it wants to know about Theodore Roosevelt. What do we know of art? We are processors of fact, not prophets of revelation. The exquisite disorder of life terrifies us, and we seek to reduce it to a neat progression of eight-by-five index cards. We are incapable of poetic rapture. About the only things we roll in a fine frenzy are microfilm machines.

Above all, book persons say, we lack the originality or the uniqueness of vision that distinguishes true artists. Small in our self-estimation, we vicariously relive the lives of large men, or, in the field of operatic biography, large women.

Well really, do book persons say all this? Not in so many words, perhaps, but they think it! Anyone who has written a serious biography—in other words, most of us here in this room—will remember that when his or her work was reviewed, there was very little discussion of the book as a book, still less of the author as an author. Indeed, the art of biography (for there is such an art) rarely admits of acknowledgment. At its best it is the art that conceals art; it is most present when it seems to be absent.

Being an art, alas, it manages to contradict anything one tries to say in definition, including what I have just said. For who is more obtrusively present, in the greatest of all biographies, than the ubiquitous Boswell? Is he an artist—or merely a celebrity maven, desperate for us to see him sitting down to coffee with Johnson? But Boswell's art is as subtle as any in the history of literature. He knew that Johnson without an interlocutor was as a cello with no strings. Those magnificent conversations, if you analyze them carefully, are written—not recorded—with a playwright's skill. Playwrights understand that nothing is less coherent than ordinary speech, accurately transcribed. Even if it is extraordinary, as Johnson's doubtless was, it will be full of longeurs, discursions, and inconsistencies, and in committing itself to paper, it will lose the inflections and gestures of real life. The playwright can be confident that these losses will be restored in performance, but Boswell was faced with the problem of making Johnson *read* the way he used to *sound*. Accordingly, when the old man was in full flood, Boswell merely dashed down stenographic notes and reconstructed the conversations later on. In doing so, he compressed for the sake of lucidity and edited for the sake of consistency.

This required art of a high order, for what resulted was artificial in the extreme. That is why the dialogues in the *Life of Johnson* seem so natural and inevitable.

And if any book persons say that by doing these things, Boswell stepped out of his bounds as a biographer and perverted the truth (rather than making it more clear), they do not understand the art of biography, which is to extract the essential from the unessential, so that truth shines forth. What is all art, indeed, but a refinement of the ore of life?

That being said, we biographers must accept that we live in a more pedantic age than Boswell. It is hardly possible to note, these days, that Scott Fitzgerald took a train somewhere without interviewing the conductor's granddaughter and sending off his ticket stub for chemical analysis. So perhaps Boswell's style and method are no longer valid. I see no reason, however, why we should not broaden our art to use the techniques of arts more fully developed than ours—fiction, above all, but also painting and photography and drama and the cinema. Scholarship is not necessarily sacrificed but can even be enhanced by the use of these techniques.

Consider how movingly Richard Holmes assembles Shelley's childhood memories into an opening-page montage, seen through the eyes of an infant. The effect is as beautiful as James Joyce's identical device in *Portrait of the Artist as a Young Man.* And surely the artist-biographer must describe Virginia Woolf's suicidal dive into the river, with a stone in her coat, in terms of that unforgettable image in *Orlando* of the old bumboat woman sitting twenty fathoms down in the frozen Thames, with her plaids and farthingales about her, and her lap full of apples. Both images—the tortured madwoman of real life, and the premonitory symbol in her own novel—cry out for imaginative synthesis. I say "cry out" because Mrs. Woolf's latest biographer does not avail himself of this artistic opportunity.

Biography has often been compared to portrait painting, but it is more closely allied to portrait photography, in that its basic composition is determined by reality. No matter what tricks of lighting or lenses are used, the subject is unavoidably, irreducibly *there.* When Edward Steichen nervously set up his camera before J. P. Morgan, the great man just sat and stared, in effect daring Steichen to make of him what he was not. So, too, does J. P. Morgan stare balefully now, through the viewfinder of the years, at Jean Strouse. I do not know how she is going to see him, but I do know what Steichen saw when he put his head under the black cloth. He saw an onrushing express train, with headlamp eyes and a cowcatcher of a nose. And that is what he photographed, so brilliantly that we recoil from his print in fear of a collision. Here is the challenge of the biographer—to restore, by whatever art he can muster, the power of the past; to make the distant seem near, the real more real.

Again, I would suggest that reality cannot truthfully be represented without honest distortions. The Greek architects who laid the Parthenon slightly out of synch were artists, in that they understood that their building would look straighter that way. We can learn from such designers how to move the reader's eye along vital lines and surfaces, how to arrest it with a show of filigree and then speed it on again to that precise central point where the whole structure balances, and the inner axis is revealed.

Biography also has much to borrow from music, particularly counterpoint and the handling of disparate motifs. Mozart composed the five themes for the finale of the *Jupiter* Symphony in such shape that, when they at last all sound at the same time, the effect is of strengthening sunlight, making clear what has gone before. So, too, the biographer who wants important themes to sound must introduce each one at the right moment in the symphony he is scoring.

Perhaps I may illustrate from a life I know quite well. Theodore Roosevelt was at least seven men—a naturalist, a soldier, a writer, and so on. I tried to introduce each of these aspects, these themes, to the reader during the course of *The Rise of Theodore Roosevelt* in such a way as to register on his mind with maximum impact. In real life, however, the themes often confusingly combined. For example, TR began his career as a ranchman before his first wife died, and continued it, off and on, long after he married his second; but I introduce the theme of Theodore Roosevelt, ranchman, after the sad chords of the former event and develop it fully before the happy fanfare of his wedding to Edith Carow. In doing so, I do not alter the chronology of history at all, any more than a composer transgresses against the regular passage of bar-lines. Nor do I boast that what I did was art: let's call it, simply, orchestration.

It was Virginia Woolf who first used the phrase "The Art of Biography," in an essay written, I think, in the 1930s. She admitted to being deeply drawn to this art—for creative rather than scholarly reasons. *Orlando*, interestingly, is subtitled *A Biography*, although it is in fact a novel about an androgynous youth who lives for hundreds of years. The author began it in February 1927, when she was badly blocked; by chance she doodled that subtitle, and, to use her own words, "No sooner had I done this than my body was flooded with rapture and my brain with ideas, and I wrote rapidly till twelve. But listen; suppose Orlando turns out to be Vita . . . ."

Of course (and she admitted it) Orlando *was* Vita Sackville-West, her sometime lesbian lover. Much of the book's ravishing imagery is directly related to the facts of Vita's life—for example, the scene where Orlando makes love meltingly to his maid on the ice is an artistic consummation of Vita's first meeting with Violet Trefusis, also on ice, that was duly recorded in Virginia's diary.

Virginia Woolf went on to write a genuine life of Roger Fry, which is, according to Leon Edel, "one of the most beautiful biographical portraits of our time." But her conclusion, alas, was that biography was not an art; it represented "life lived at a lower degree of tension" than fiction or poetry. In a devastating passage she wrote:

> The artist's imagination at its most intense fires out what is perishable in fact; he builds with what is durable; but the biographer must accept the perishable, build with it, imbed it in the very fabric of his work. Much will perish; little will live. And thus we come to the conclusion that he is a craftsman, not an artist; and his work is not a work of art, but something betwixt and between.

She said that, despite Boswell and Lockhart, there are no "immortal" biographies. Mr. Micawber would survive Lytton Strachey's *Queen Victoria.*

This may be true, although there is at least as much of Dickens's father in Mr. Micawber as there is of the real Queen in Strachey's book. We cannot deny, however, that Dickens had the luxury of combining his original with other originals, real or imaginary, in proportions known only to himself; this luxury, this freedom to invent, is the essential difference between the novelist and the biographer. Indeed, were we given such pure oxygen to breathe, we would become giddy. Let us confess that the greatest triumphs of the creative imagination will always outsoar our own more shackled art. But let us also remember the greatest biographies themselves outsoar 99 percent of the rest of literature. Strachey's *Queen*

Victoria is superior to countless thousands, perhaps millions, of ephemeral novels, and to this day I can think of no work of fiction that closes as poignantly. Is not Shakespeare's Henry V vastly more interesting than many of his purely imaginary characters? Painter's Proust is to some tastes better than Proust's Proust. Scott is almost impossible to read these days, but Lockhart is still inexhaustibly interesting.

In claiming that biography may improve itself by absorbing the finest elements of the imaginative arts (always remaining within the membrane of scholarship), I do not suggest that any reverse osmosis can be to the benefit of fiction. "Faction," to use the current grotesquery, combines the worst elements of each—biography's lack of invention and fiction's lack of responsibility. If we wish to know all about Gary Gillmore, do we really want him novelized for easier consumption? When we buy a new Philip Roth novel, do we not hope against hope that it will not be another volume of his ongoing memoirs, complete with medical reports? Increasingly we are disappointed.

By the same token, in my opinion, biographers should stay away from Freud. Let novelists like D. M. Thomas discover, to general delight, that the good doctor has more to offer their art than ours. Here, I realize, I begin to tread on difficult ground, for our ranks abound with psychobiographers, some of whom—Leon Edel comes to mind—are distinguished authors of distinguished books. Yet I cannot rid myself of Scott Fitzgerald's notion that "action is character," even more in biography than in fiction. If action is presented characteristically enough, no intrusive analyzing on the part of the narrator is necessary. The ideal biographer should be godlike in the Flaubertian sense—apparent everywhere, visible nowhere. Or to compare him once again to the photographer, let him arrange every frame to his satisfaction; after he has done so, let him step out of the picture, and take his shadow with him.

When the modern biographer disobeys this elementary rule of good composition—which is to say good narrative—the results are almost always unfortunate, particularly in the field of historical biography. History is a memory, a dream; any harsh voice from the present jerks us awake, to our discomfort. Philip Ziegler, the recent biographer of Lord Melbourne, has a voice more mellifluous than harsh, yet it intrudes all the same, destroying the spell that Lord David Cecil cast so enchantingly in *Melbourne* (1939). In a gracious foreword, Mr. Ziegler explains why he has presumed to rewrite "one of the most delightful biographies of our age." Much new material has come to light—many thousands of letters, and a large fragment of Melbourne's own autobiography. Mr. Ziegler also confesses he could never understand how Lord David's Melbourne, "a man so insouciant, detached, and free from ambition," could have prevailed so in politics. His vision, then, is much more ruthless and grainy—authentically 1970ish. "Every biographer perhaps to some extent," he hazards, "is a victim of his generation and of his prejudices. If so, Lord David has enjoyed incomparably the happier lot. But, almost regretfully, I fear that I am right."

His portrait of Lady Caroline Lamb also suffers from this kind of presentism. It is relentlessly editorial, despite its dictum: "To be eschewed, however, is the temptation to apply modern psycho-analytic techniques to the scraps of information which survive about her and thus to arrive at some glib formula which would 'explain' her as a textbook of the latest fashionable neurosis." Lord David, one feels, would have eschewed both the psychoanalysis and the conversational aside. Of the forty-four descriptive sentences Mr. Ziegler proceeds to give Lady Caroline, seventeen contain subjective inflections and mood-shattering remarks. His portrait is not without charm—"her eyes perpetually smudged as if she had just been crying or intended soon to do so"—but let us check Lord David's. It has not one personal opinion in twenty-five sentences. It is, surprisingly, less romantic than Mr. Ziegler's, and more psychologically penetrating—instead of giving us his inferences, he quotes self-revelatory letters. It is also, because Lord David does not step with tweeds and a pipe into Lady Caroline's satin drawing room, more elegant and more vivid. These adjectives apply throughout to his portrait of Lord Melbourne ("smiling, indolent and inscrutable he lay, a pawn in the hands of fortune") and of course his prologue is one of the great set pieces of English biographical exposition.

Lytton Strachey remarked that biography is "the most delicate and humane of all the branches of the art of writing." It would be vain to accept his superlative, but it would be folly to ignore his scruples: delicacy and humaneness must lie at the heart of our work, if we wish it to survive as art.

THE YEAR OF THE
BIOGRAPHY

ON THE ●CBS TELEVISION NETWORK

1. Jack Dempsey
Possibly the most popular American prizefighter ever, Jack Dempsey was the toast of the boxing world in the 1920s. This show captures the young Dempsey as he strikes to become the heavyweight champion of the world.

2. Babe: On His Own
Babe Didrikson Zaharias, known to this production but still a child. Mentally retarded from birth, he was institutionalized for forty-six years before meeting one Mac Driscoll (Lou City hero) with two sides of unusual people. This presentation, based on part of the real Bill his love's life, portrays his struggle to make a life for himself with the help of Mac and others who care about him.

3. Cook and Peary
By the turn of the century, explorers were seriously attempting to reach the North Pole, one of the remaining uncharted portions of the globe. This program centers its attention on the efforts of Dr. Frederick Cook to reclaim Lieutenant Robert Peary, the preeminent explorer of his day, to the top of the world.

4. Calamity Jane
Martha Jane Canary, better known as "Calamity Jane," was as much a mythic creature of the American West as Wyatt Earp or Jesse James. Her indomitable spirit led her into numerous adventures, which are explored in this dramatization of an original screenplay based on Canary's riddles and letters to her daughter.

5. Anatomy of an Illness
Norman Cousins, dynamic editor of the Saturday Review, was stricken with multiplying spondylitis—a degenerative spinal condition—in the mid 1960s. This show dramatizes that event. Cousins' unique self-treatment and the effects on his family and friends.

6. John Paul II
This program focuses on the charismatic, dedicated Pontiff from the days of his youth as Karol Wojtyla in Wadowice, Poland, to his installation as head of the world's Roman Catholic Church. The drama includes his years in his native country as a religious leader, diplomat, social activist against the Nazi regime and strong adversary of the communist government.

7. George Washington
George Washington, leader of the Continental Army during the American Revolution and first president of the United States, is often portrayed on a larger than life figure in American history. This eight-hour mini-series, based on James Flexner's biography, attempts to show the human side behind the man considered the "father of his country."

36

What is Biography?

A Discussion

📖 Questions and comments were invited from members of the audience. Topics in the wide-ranging discussion that followed included biography as art, biography and psychoanalysis, the importance of putting lives in the context of their times, biography's popularity (one view was, "It's fun to read other people's mail"), the common mistake of assuming any biography is definitive, and the relationship of biography to history and fiction. A sampling of the comments follows.

EDMUND MORRIS
"The personality of a biographer should not intrude into a narrative. The only way to achieve a real transparency of style is to go back to your work and ruthlessly cut out personal opinions and prejudices. . . . Of course one cannot write a biography without constantly psychoanalyzing one's subject, but one should not do so nakedly and obviously."

◀ This poster, commissioned by CBS Television to mark the broadcast of seven television biographies during the 1983/84 season, was designed by graphic artist Robert Hess. The figures depicted are (*clockwise from the lower left*) North Pole explorers Frederick Cook and Robert Peary, Bill Sackler (portrayed by Mickey Rooney), Norman Cousins (portrayed by Ed Asner), George Washington, Pope John Paul II (portrayed by Albert Finney), Calamity Jane, and Jack Dempsey. Reading lists for the seven biography television specials were prepared by the Library of Congress as part of the CBS Television/Library of Congress "Read More About It" book project.

MARC
PACHTER

"In evolving a notion of biography as an art, we are trying to get it away from its earlier function, which was to categorize people according to a theory rather than to let the life follow its own pattern. This is a key distinction (and problem): can the artist-biographer allow the life to control its own destiny to a certain extent and still create a book that has a beginning, a middle, and an end? . . . When a systematic theory—Freudian, Marxist, or whatever—predominates over the life, you have the antithesis of an artful biography."

ANNE
FREEDGOOD

"There isn't any such thing as a totally detached biographer. All biography comes from a point of view. You cannot get away from it. . . . The question is whether a biographer confesses or instead presents the facts in such a way that people will accept (the biographer's) point of view."

Speaker Samuel S. Vaughan (center) with Jo Vaughan and Townsend Hoopes, biographer of John Foster Dulles and president of the Association of American Publishers.

John Y. Cole introduces the discussion about biography in print and on film. Librarian of Congress Daniel J. Boorstin is in the center, and CBS Senior Vice President David Fuchs on the right.

Speaker Edmund Morris responds to a question from the audience.

Biographers Robert A. Caro and Anne Edwards with editor Anne
Freedgood.

RONNIE
DUGGER

"I have vast appreciation for the practice of
biography as an art . . . but I'm uncomfortable
with that formulation if it's categorical or
implicit in its intention. . . . What attracts me
to biography is curiosity about the relationship
between human nature, social process, and the
future of society. We are puzzled about how
we are governed and about the relationship
between the personality in the successful figures and the systems they are part of."

KENNETH
LYNN

"The current state of the novel helps account
for the increased popularity of biography.
Novels no longer tell stories or portray characters, and we have an appetite, a need for
these things that biography helps meet. The
situation inside the university also explains the
rise and popularity of biography. There is an
animus against the individual in both English

and history departments. In English departments there is a decline in interest in literary history and a decline in interest in authors as such. The fashion is to take literary intentions as well as their lives away from authors. And in history, there is no longer any kind of interest in the individual. Political history is in disgrace, social history is *it*, and it's a social history of anonymous groups. So neither professors of English nor professors of history are meeting this need."

W. JACKSON BATE

"The high quality of biography now—and I think it is higher on the average than at the beginning of the century—is partly a result, as Kenneth Lynn suggests, of the change in the character of the novel. Those great nineteenth-century novels were at their best when they were giving the educational development of the characters, which was done in a rich social context. Today there is a tendency both in historical and literary academic studies to dehumanize the subject; people are more interested in methodology than in the humanistic side, narrative or psychological. Biography has stepped into the breech as the novel has become more self-conscious. . . . In many ways, biography has replaced the Victorian novel."

JEAN STROUSE

"Biography has changed a great deal in the last 100 years. Major biographies in the nineteenth century tended to describe exemplary lives; . . . now we are interested in quite different questions, such as motive, what sort of person this was, and what those intersections of history and private life were (that contributed) to the process of moral development. Psychoanalysis gives us new ways of thinking about these questions.

41

George Nash, biographer of Herbert Hoover, queries literary biographer W. Jackson Bate.

A. Scott Berg and Thomas B. Congdon, who edited Berg's biography of Max Perkins.

Symposium speaker David McCullough, a biographer of Theodore
Roosevelt and Harry Truman, speaks with Robert Massie, whose most
recent biography is about Peter the Great.

ERNEST
SAMUELS
"The biographer tries to compress a chrono-
logical movement through time, yet on the
page that life is simply 'there,' line by line.
The biographer therefore is *responsible* to that
life, for making it live by staying focused on
the life itself."

ROBERT
MASSIE
"Since biography has such great across-the-
board appeal, I encourage more universities
to let biographers teach courses about biography . . . and to introduce students to history
that is readable. Biography is a superb way to
illuminate the past and I don't think it should
be left entirely to historians."

SAMUEL S.
VAUGHAN

"As a publisher, I'm puzzled by biography. It does not sell as well, as a category, as one might expect. . . . I don't trust the polls about reading habits. Men respond by saying they read biography because they think it's justifiable—not time-wasting like poetry or fiction. But I suspect that many men are really exhibitionist readers of biography and closet readers of fiction."

ERWIN
GLIKES

"Biography, I think, is what we will be reading and wanting to read in the 1980s. . . . Readers want to know the meaning of individual lives rather than all the depressing theories about the meaninglessness of individual life. Biography is rescuing minds and lives from the social sciences, and it is doing so in an absolutely brilliant way. Our best biographers are accomplished social scientists—they know how to evaluate materials, and they understand psychoanalysis and make use of what has been done in political science and elsewhere. But our readers are not scholarly. They are living human beings who want to know the answer to one thing—What does it all mean? What is the meaning of 'going on?' They want to know the story, and the story implies meaning. . . . It seems to me that it is not the history of nations or great tendencies or political movements or demographic characteristics that will survive in the 1980s—it's going to be the individual life reexamined for meaning, even if that meaning is very lightly or delicately hinted at."

The symposium audience: biographers, publishers, editors, librarians,
and readers.

Actor Barry Bostwick and author James Flexner celebrate the completion of the CBS Television miniseries on George Washington, which featured Bostwick and was based on Flexner's biography.

EDITOR'S NOTE   The "Books & Biography" symposium included a discussion on the evening of November 9, 1983, about biography in print and on film. The forthcoming CBS Television miniseries on George Washington, based on James Thomas Flexner's biography, was the focal point. The series, one of fifteen television specials in the 1983–84 CBS/Library of Congress "Read More About It" project, concluded with a thirty-second message about reading from actor Barry Bostwick, who played George Washington. At the symposium, Mr. Flexner and producer/writer Richard Fielder discussed the adaptation of the book for television, and Barry Bostwick described how it felt to portray the Father of his Country. The remarks of Mr. Flexner follow.

George Washington in Print and on Television

James Thomas Flexner

📖 Since I have been assigned to talk about my biographies of Washington in relation to the television play that is based upon them, I must first define the volumes themselves. I started out with the idea of writing a one-volume biography, but finding the subject so rich and so complicated, I ended up with four volumes that were published between 1965 and 1972. Then I decided that by hitting the high spots and relying on the four volumes to supply documentation and greater depth, I could do one volume after all, which I called *The Indispensable Man*. The television script, however, as has been pointed out in almost every public statement that has been made about it, is based on the larger set, particularly the first two volumes. We all hope for another show, based on the last two.

Before I began my labors on Washington, I had published eleven books on American history and biography, and Washington made a small or a large appearance in many of these. It was as though I had met him again and again, each time in a different social milieu. I became fascinated by the fact that the man I encountered was never the man described in the books I read. I decided that when I was old enough I would write a biography of Washington. Then, the distinguished publishers Little, Brown quite independently asked me to write such a life, and I decided I was old enough.

When I told people that I was working on Washington, I was almost invariably asked how, after two centuries, there could possibly be anything new to say. Had I uncovered a mass of new source material? As it turned out I was to discover a good many new documents, some important, but that was not the point. The emphasis placed on new documentation is an aspect of conventional scholarship that too often results in distortion. The discovery tends to be emphasized by the discoverer out of all proportion to its role in the entire record.

My intention was to read every known document—whenever it was found and however seemingly trivial—that Washington had written, and also all other papers that Washington's acts or correspondence indicated would prove significant to his career. Of course, although this is often overlooked by documentary historians in their search of what they consider hard facts, hardly anything a man writes fails to reveal aspects of his character. It was my hope, as it has been for all of my books, to join in a coherent narrative both personality and the events that shaped or were shaped by that personality.

At the start, I resolved to clear from my mind, by an act of will, everything I had previously heard about Washington: I did not know whether he was a genius or a pompous dullard, whether he was a noble or an evil man. Thus, by a stroke of will, I banished all the myths and misunderstanding, special pleadings, social theories (usually contemporary to the times of their origins), all the venal and crackbrained anecdotes that have accreted around Washington down the generations. The losses of valuable insights that might result from my working plan could be considerably ameliorated by recourse to Douglas Southall Freeman's monumental seven-volume life of Washington. Since that work was built by a brilliant scholar on material gathered by a large foundation-supported team, I could use Freeman's source references as divining rods to point at the best among the many, many thousands of secondary sources. And my method of starting, as it were, anew did give me the tremendous advantage, which is reflected in the television script, of viewing Washington with fresh, unencumbered eyes.

The devil did dangle a lucrative possibility before me.

Particularly when I was writing on Washington and the American Revolution at the time of the Vietnam war, there was great pressure on me to dwell on parallels. Had I been willing to do so, I could have appeared on the best talk shows—I was invited—and could have relied on at least doubling the sale of my book. But had I given in to pressures to make my work, as it was put, "contemporary," the biography would be out of date now, and the current show would never have existed. The script and the subsequent acting have preserved the tone I maintained of adhering to eighteenth-century realities without any distortions or detours undertaken to reflect contemporary issues.

I pursued my research and my writing unblinkingly, without suppressing anything. Fortunately, there was in the Washington record nothing grievous to suppress. I moved so far from the accepted marble image, however, that I foresaw attacks from conservative patriots. As it turns out, the conservatives fell in behind me because they were glad to have the father of our country presented as a man whom other human beings could love and admire. The attacks came from the left, from radicals who wished to tear down American institutions and thus resented having Washington depicted as anything but a bugaboo.

Actually, although the presentation of Washington in my books and in the television script seems today to be a novelty, it is far from being that. Understandably, considering my method, which carried me back altogether into the eighteenth century, I ended up with the evaluation of Washington, both as a person and as a public figure, which was that of his contemporaries, agreed to, after his death, even by those who had been violently opposed to him. Starting from an impartial position, I concluded that Washington was both lovable and one of the greatest leaders in the history of the world.

As my volumes were published, one after another, they were subjected to a certain amount of sniping, but they were, considering their departure from contemporary convention, made surprisingly welcome. Even the Washington-haters did not mount a coherent opposition. I received a Pulitzer prize and a National Book Award. Sales, although not tremendous, were respectable and continuous. I was, of course, gratified, but wished that what I believed was the truth about Washington could travel beyond readers of serious books. Then I heard from my lawyer that a producer named David Gerber wished to buy television rights.

The most common question I am now asked is how far I have had the power to control the television presentation. The question is fundamentally a naive one, since contract provisions of that nature cannot in practice, except in extreme cases, be enforced. I, myself, have no legal right whatsoever to dictate to anyone concerned with the production. Yet I have been consulted to a degree which, considering the experiences of many of my friends, is remarkable. The basis for cooperation has been a meeting of minds among people who have, each in his own sphere, the same objectives, who have come to like and, most importantly, respect each other.

I was not consulted at first, which may well have been an advantage, as I would probably have objected to the great emphasis that was being placed on Washington's life before the Revolution. But when I saw the script for the first two hours I realized how well these early years, when he was not pressed by great events, were being used to depict Washington's character.

I took it upon myself to send the scriptwriter, Richard Fielder, a long series of suggestions, both large and small, even presuming to give advice not only on factual matters but as a fellow writer. Instead of being annoyed, Fielder felt I was being helpful. We had considerable back and forth both by mail and by telephone, and eventually he came to New York and we went over the final script together, line by line. We ended up with the fewest possible number of disagreements.

It is proverbial that historical consultants and television writers get into confrontations that are damaging to the result, however they are resolved. One reason that Fielder and I got on so well was, I am sure, because we are both members of what the English historian J. H. Plumb calls "the republic of letters." He respected me in my line, and I respected him in his. I had, indeed, in my younger days written some television dramas that were aired by CBS—as part of the Omnibus show, supported by the Ford Foundation—and I was conscious of how the playwright's art differed from the book writer's. The playwright has actors as additional tools and can make use of silence, something that is closed to a book writer. It is very difficult, however, for the playwright to express general ideas without elaborate and time-consuming dramatization or soliloquies that bring action to a halt. Fielder and his colleagues opposed having an introducer like Alistair Cook— I confess I fancied myself in that role—or any voice-over. They argued that either would keep his play from standing on its own as a work of art.

Basic to my agreement with Dick Fielder and many others was a shared sense of dedication to what we all feel is a noble cause. As the project grew with production, this conviction went beyond Fielder to the producer, David Gerber, the director, Buzz Kulik, whom I have come to regard as my good friend, Barry Bostwick, who plays Washington, and the other actors, who have not only listened to my advice but asked for it, the executives at General Motors and their advertising agency, N.W. Ayer, and the personnel involved at CBS. We all felt that we were in a position to make a real contribution to American life.

Behind the almost evangelical air that sometimes seemed to prevail as the screening went on is a conviction that the fundamental values of the founding fathers are invaluable today in the United States—and, indeed, the world—and are under serious attack. We are engaging in no propaganda or arguments but are aiming to present the truth in one specific but vital area. We are trying to give back to America the Father of Our Country as the person he actually was.

The television show we have in preparation is not a history lesson, although it may well propel thousands of Americans to such lessons. It is an effort to delineate truthfully the character of a man who occupies a place in every American psyche, who is more than any other the human embodiment of the American flag. Away with the fallacious cherry tree, with wooden false teeth that never existed! We hope to reveal, in his youth and middle age, a man who was known in his own generation as "amiable," possessed of charm and magnetism and great physical prowess. A man who taught himself to be the person his highest ideals made him wish to be, who learned from experience to be a triumphant general and had within himself the possibility to become, as president, a leader for all the world to follow toward freedom, the democratic process, and the self-determination of peoples. A man who, although assaulted like all of us with the temptations of flesh and ego, achieved, through willpower and magnanimity, a greatness that when fully revealed will shine as a guiding light down the years.

Biography in the City of Washington

David McCullough

📖 Early in the century the English writer J. B. Priestley paid a visit to the United States during which he went to see the Grand Canyon. To his amazement he discovered that the canyon is part of our National Park Service. "Every federal employee," he said, "should remind himself with triumphant pride that he serves on the staff of the Grand Canyon." I think that is something we might also say for the Library of Congress.

What a possession for a country is this great institution. It really ought to be called the National Library, for that is what it is. Speaking for myself, I doubt I could survive in my work without the Library of Congress. My work began here. All of my books have been dependent on the resources of this Library and its staff.

My mistake in the early days was to go into this and other libraries trying to cover up how much I didn't know—such as how to use a library. But I learned the more I worked that the best approach is to be as open as possible about how much you don't know and to throw your fate at the feet of these wonderful, helpful people. Miracles will begin to happen.

The Library has, I am told, 20 million books. Its shelf space runs to 540 miles, if you can imagine such a thing, which is like trying to comprehend the scale of the Grand Canyon. The Library is also filled with marvelous collections that have been largely untapped—manuscript collections, for example, that are waiting for biographers. I will mention just two. One is the James G. Blaine collection. What a story he is! (His house, as you may know, still stands at Dupont

Circle.) And all the papers of this extraordinary, colorful, very important American politician and superb subject for a writer are waiting for a writer.

Another example is the collection of Agnes Ernst Meyer, wife of Eugene Meyer, the Eugene Meyer of the *Washington Post*, and mother of Katherine Graham. Agnes Meyer knew everybody and she knew everything. She came from a poor Lutheran family in New York and married a wealthy, ambitious Jewish publisher. If there ever was a story, it's right there. And the papers are all waiting.

The problem, of course, is that we who work in the field are limited in our time and energies. So if we cannot write all the books we want to, we should do more to spread the word to those looking for subjects, be they editors or authors.

I came to Washington originally during the Kennedy administration to work under Edward R. Murrow when he was running the U.S. Information Agency. Since then I have had feelings about the city that I will try to explain.

I do not think there should be a great differentiation, a great dividing line, between biographers and historians and novelists and poets. I firmly believe we are writers, and a good writer ought to be able to write *anything*. I would like to write a play sometime. I would like to write a novel. I would like to write biography, history. I am not trained in scholarship. I am not trained in biography or anything else, and I am not sure there is a proper training for a writer, except possibly to run off with the circus at an early age. That might be excellent training. I think, however, that we do best when we go where the material is. We need so much more than we use—ten, twenty times more—because we have to be so selective. And here in Washington we have, easily, the greatest concentration of library and archival facilities in the country, if not the world.

There are collections I never knew of until recently, collections so good, so rich, so full of possibilities that it is more than enough to make you want to get up out of bed very early in the morning. The Archives of American Art at the Smithsonian, for example, has a wonderful collection of oral histories and original papers of American painters. The Martin Luther King Library now has all of the morgue files of the *Washington Star*. Imagine. It also has a collection of Frederic J. Haskin, who began writing a syndicated question-and-answer column in 1916. He received over a thousand letters a day. That material is all at the Martin Luther King Library. I have brought two examples. One is from Northampton, Massachusetts, dated November 4, 1929. It is signed by Calvin Coolidge:

Dear Sir:
I do not feel that I have any favorite songs of which I can give you a list. Cordially yours.

The second is from Miss Helen Dukas, secretary to Professor Einstein, dated December 5, 1946:

Dear Sir:
Professor Einstein wants me to acknowledge the receipt of your letter and to inform you that he never submitted to the so-called IQ test because he did not want to take the risk.

There is an institution here known as the Columbia Historical Society, which has an incomparable collection of social history, records of social life at every level in Washington, going all the way back. There is the Georgetown Library. There is the Ralph Bunche Collection of Oral History at Howard University dealing with the civil rights movement. There is, of course, the National Archives. In the years when I was writing *The Path between the Seas*, I spent weeks working with the National Archives collections at Suitland, Maryland. And I would like to emphasize that working with such great collections does not just provide you with things to know, it provides you with things to feel, which can be more important.

I wondered at one point, for example, if there might be records from the old, French Canal hospital of those who died of yellow fever and malaria. Somebody went downstairs, or wherever they go, and brought back several boxes. I opened one of the boxes and there, like bundles of old bonds or bills, were the death certificates of the people who died in that hospital. For the first time I really felt what a terrifying time it must have been, what courage there was in that pioneering venture.

The Library of Congress, however, is the perfect model, it seems to me, not just of the volume but of the diversity of material to be found in Washington. We need quantity but we also need quality, and we need quality in many fields. We need good maps. We need to look at photographs.

I am working now on a biography of Harry Truman. In the Library of Congress there is a marvelous photograph of Independence Square taken around the turn of the century by an itinerant photographer of the kind who were doing one town square after another all through the Middle West. The square is usually a panorama—one hundred and eighty degrees, comprised of several photographs stitched together—and when this is spread out on a desk and you have a magnifying glass, you can spend the better part of the day studying it all and gaining material of a kind not to be found any other way. It is almost as good as being there. Since Truman as a boy worked in a drugstore on Independence Square and since the square with its courthouse and all its courthouse loafers was the vital center of things through a good part of his political life, this is an extremely important set, or setting, for the story.

Among the greatest settings for many of us has been this very city. Washington is the place where so many of our stories take place. I sometimes walk the city in a bit of a daze, I suppose, seeing things that aren't there. I go by the White House and see Jefferson walking on the lawn with Alexander Von Humboldt in 1804—two of the most remarkable men of the last century—talking, talking, talking endlessly about every imaginable subject. Humboldt had just returned from his epic expedition through Central and South America, an expedition that made the Lewis and Clark trek look like a light outing. I go by the Treasury Department in the winter when snow is on the roof, and I try to imagine Theodore Roosevelt, Sr., scaling the roof to measure it for skylights— the Roosevelts being then in the glass business—and to imagine the joy he had sliding down the roof, as he said, as if he were an Alpine climber. I stand at the corner of L and Vermont with all its traffic and modern buildings, and I think of Walt Whitman standing there watching Lincoln go by on his grey horse with his accompanying cavalry in bright uniforms, and Lincoln looking very dark and ordinary, as Whitman wrote, but exchanging glances with Whitman.

Whitman, of course, lived here and wrote here, and wrote powerfully of the war and the suffering. We have Washington authors of the same era as different from Whitman as Henry Adams. We have authors in the White House as different from Lincoln as Woodrow Wilson, and, more recently, authors as different as Dean Acheson and Rachel Carson. This is a writer's city. It's a story city.

We all know how much we have been moved, and in some cases, inspired by the writing we have read about this city by our contemporaries. I think of Robert Caro's brilliant description of Lyndon Johnson arriving in Washington and going to the Capitol. Or of Barbara Tuchman's superb first chapter in *The Proud Tower*, her portrait of Speaker Reed, which is something we should take out and read every once in a while to remind ourselves how good we can be in this business.

My own favorite is in *Reveille in Washington*, the opening pages where Margaret Leech describes poor old Winfield Scott, in his ponderous, declining glory. I think it was when I read that that I began to sense what opportunity for writing there is in the past.

The city is the shrine of the government of the *people*, by the *people*, for the *people*, as Carl Sandburg taught us to say, and it is everywhere you turn a hymn, a tribute, to the individual. There are temples to individuals—Lincoln, Jefferson. There are statues everywhere we turn—of John Kennedy, Hiawatha, Queen Isabella, Albert Einstein, Winston Churchill, not to mention more of Jefferson and Lincoln. Indeed, if there is one individual who dominates the city, it is not the man for whom it is named, it is Lincoln. He is everywhere— the Memorial, Ford's Theatre, the Peterson House where he died, the great portrait by Healy that dominates the hall of presidents at the National Portrait Gallery. He is out at the

Soldier's Home, he is in ten to a dozen statues and other paintings around the city. He's here. I suppose you could also say the dome on the Capitol is Lincoln: "It must be built," he insisted, while the war continued.

But more important even than such symbols, the city also provides us with the living models we ought to be looking at as closely as we look at the written record—as a paleontologist will go and find the living organism to better understand the fossil record. If we are writing about a prima donna, be he politician or bureaucrat, we should be taking a look at that variety, never in short supply here. If we are writing about Washington's social butterflies—or social moths as Harry Truman called them—we should be observing them. I don't think many historians and biographers observe life very well, life today, in our present. I don't think they see as much as they should. We need to work with the living model as much as possible. We need to look out the window more than we do, to mull more. People are very hard to know . . . in our daily life, in our household, in our place of work, very hard to know.

Now, surely, one of the joys of our work is to get inside another way of life, another vocation. And, again, in this city we have the resources to do that because of all the professions represented here, either by professional organizations or by the living examples—medicine, engineering, military, politics, the law, and on and on. It is rightfully a mecca for those of us in the writer's trade, and the fact that the press is so important here should be important to those of us who write history, because we ought to think how well, not how badly, they do their job. They haven't the time to sit around and consider, reflect, and write and rewrite, as we do. They have to get it out, every day. That they are as accurate, perceptive, and sometimes as clairvoyant as they are is, to me, miraculous. I never worked on a newspaper; I wish I had.

We are going to see more biography written, surely. It is probably going to get better, because I expect we are going to open our perspective and take the blinders off. We will be looking at a great deal more than just politics and the military, the traditional preoccupations of so much history and biography. For a long time our history and biography have been essentially a celebration of the state, because we were a new state, a new country. When Humboldt came to visit Jefferson in 1804, Jefferson wrote him a letter saying, in effect (and this was only in the last century) "you might wish to think twice about coming here, because there's really nothing much here to see." "Nothing curious," he said. He was excluding himself apparently. How very different today. We are interested now in other areas of our enterprise—our imagination, our initiative, our pioneering—beyond politics and the military. And certainly one of the areas that we must all start looking at is the impact of science and technology on our history. When Jefferson and Humboldt were walking around the White House lawn, they represented the essence, the ultimate in nineteenth-century science at that time. In the twenty years after the Civil War, the time when John Wesley Powell and Clarence King were living in Washington, the city became an important world center for science, which suggests how relatively small and unimportant the world of science then was.

The most important news of our century, in my view, was announced in this city on January 26, 1939, in a classroom on the second floor of a building that still stands at George Washington University. The announcement typifies the little-known present—nobody paid much attention to it. Life went on. It was another several years before anyone began to realize what had been made known. If you need to be reminded of the importance of science and technology and what goes on in this city, let me just describe what happened in that room. The shy and rather soft-spoken Dane, Niels Bohr, announced that the uranium atom, if split, would produce a power millions of times greater than anything known on earth. There were a number of theoretical physicists in the room and a few reporters. The reporters sat looking around thinking, well, what else are they going to say? The physicists, normally rather well controlled, staid people, jumped up from their chairs and rushed to the nearest telephones—just like reporters—to call Johns Hopkins, to call the Carnegie Institution, to call all the places around the country where the atom smashers were. All Thursday night, in laboratories, in classrooms, and in studies around the country, the work went on. Saturday night, back here in Washington, came the word. It was true. And the world has never been the same.

Harry Truman said, "The only new thing in the world is the history you don't know." He was wrong, because *that* was new. And I don't know of a more productive and constantly renewing source for a writer of history and biography than this our capital city.

Biographers and Their Subjects

A Summary of Discussion and Comment

📖 After his presentation, David McCullough was joined by Jean Strouse and James R. Mellow for a discussion about biography behind the scenes: how writers, editors, and publishers create biography. Each addressed two questions posed by the moderator: How do you pick your subject, and How important is it that biographers like their subjects? A second set of informal presentations paired A. Scott Berg, author of *Max Perkins: Editor of Genius* (New York: E.P. Dutton, 1978), with his editor, Thomas B. Congdon, who discovered the author and his manuscript in 1973 and later published the book. A final presentation by Sylvia Morris, biographer of Edith Kermit Roosevelt (1861–1948) and Clare Boothe Luce (1903–), stimulated discussion about the advantages and pitfalls of writing about subjects who are alive. Here is a sampling of comments about biographers and their subjects.

James R. Mellow's interest in Gertrude Stein was inspired by *The Autobiography of Alice B. Toklas*, a "joyous account of the creative act." But he found his true subject "when I discovered the nineteenth century." He especially enjoys writing group portraits that examine literary figures in the context of their various friends and influences.

Jean Strouse's discovery of her subjects, Alice James and J. P. Morgan, occurred only after long and careful searches. It took her four years to settle on Morgan, her current subject. She noted that Frederick Lewis Allen's 1949 biography of Morgan is "an exquisite book," but that it "doesn't speak to us today. . . . Each age asks different questions." She sees a "complicated chemistry" between biographer and subject, but some distance is necessary, and this means that biographers do not necessarily have to like their subjects.

David McCullough has chosen subjects himself and accepted suggestions from editors. He decided not to write a biography of Picasso when asked by an editor, because he found the artist's life was not a sufficient story and, after preliminary research, he discovered he simply did not like Picasso.

Samuel S. Schoenbaum fell in love first with Shakespeare the dramatist when, as a high school student, he saw a Broadway production of Othello starring Paul Robeson, a performance "that remains as vivid as though I had just seen it."

Scott Berg's biography of Max Perkins was inspired by his infatuation with F. Scott Fitzgerald and other American writers who worked with Perkins, by encouragement from Carlos Baker, his adviser at Princeton University, and by the availability of so much rich Perkins correspondence in Princeton's Firestone Library.

Source material for biographical research, the value and uses of bibliographical notes, the detection of false clues left behind by self-conscious subjects, editors as sources of insight, oral history, and how a writer begins a biography were among the other topics of discussion. Robert Hill, editor of the Marcus Garvey papers and currently at work on a biography of Garvey, pointed out that manuscript and other source materials "very often *determine* the success of a biography— both the form it takes and its ultimate accomplishment." Adele Hast, editor-in-chief of Marquis Who's Who, Inc., described how the computer is opening up new methodologies, approaches, and source materials for biographers. She also characterized bibliographical notes as "sources of inspiration" for other biographers. Kenneth McCormick described his experiences editing the memoirs of both Harry Truman and Dwight D. Eisenhower. In Truman's case, his task was eased once he realized that, for Harry Truman, his wife Bess was "true north." He described Truman's love of reading biography. When asked if he read himself asleep with the stack of biographies that was inevitably next to his bed, the former president replied: "No, I read myself awake."

How does a biographer convey enthusiasm for a life, making the mind of the reader come alive to a personality? Good writing is essential, but so is good organization. Scott Berg, writing about a relatively unknown figure, needed a strong opening that would quickly indicate the significance of his subject. His model was a personal favorite: the parade of kings, the funeral procession of Edward VII that opens Barbara Tuchman's *Guns of August*. A Columbia University speech by Max Perkins late in his life became his own opening, his "parade of kings." But above all, the biographer must follow editor Thomas Congdon's advice to young Scott Berg: "tell stories."

SOME WRITTEN COMMENTS

Four biographers provided written insights about their experiences. Quotations from their letters are used here with their permission.

W. A. SWANBERG, biographer of Theodore Dreiser, Henry R. Luce, William Randolph Hearst, and Norman Thomas, in a letter to Daniel J. Boorstin, dated September 19, 1983:

I found it difficult to make judgments of a subject's shortcomings. To attempt Christlike understanding could be boring and evasive, but one must not carp, and simple fairness seemed the best course.

Years ago I failed in this respect in a biography of Theodore Dreiser. Although the book was well received, and has since become standard college reading, fairness came hard because of Dreiser's selfishness, anti-Semitism and plain dishonesty in some dealings. These qualities— relieved as they were by intervals of creative triumph and geniality—actually made him a more fascinating character.

But they wore me down, reduced the satisfaction I took in the work and even made me consider dropping the subject. I think my attitude shows in the book in an occasional high-and-mighty tone of disdain.

I had less trouble with a later subject, Henry R. Luce. His strong sense of mission led him to perfect a journalistic system of news-manipulation calculated to influence the nation in religio-political directions he felt essential for U.S. hegemony and hence the good of the world. His confidence in his duty as a high collaborator of the Almighty so prejudiced his journalistic treatment of individuals and movements he thought unworthy, and caused such puffery of those he approved, that the documentation of his journalism (which was the greater part of his life) was comparatively simple and painless.

Even so, I felt best of all when I finished a book on Norman Thomas, a man I so admired for his absolute integrity that it was a great pleasure to make the effort to illuminate his life and work as they deserved.

I should add that the book sold rather poorly!

FORREST G. POGUE, biographer of George C. Marshall, in a letter to Daniel J. Boorstin, August 18, 1983:

On the day after I saw General Marshall receive the Nobel Prize for Peace at Oslo, I wrote him to say that if he persisted in the course of declining to write his memoirs, I hoped he would talk to an oral historian. I said that I was one of several people who would be willing to conduct the interviews. He replied that he thought it better not to give interviews. But his secretary and aide remembered and recalled that I had mentioned my work as a combat historian in Europe in 1944–45 and the amount of interviewing I had done on the official army volume on Eisenhower in northwestern Europe, *The Supreme Command*.

In 1956 when plans were made to build a Marshall Library at V.M.I. and John D. Rockefeller, Jr., gave funds to start the collection of Marshall's papers, friends of the

General pressed him to give interviews and he agreed, provided that a group of historians recommend someone trained for this kind of work and that no money coming from such a project was to come to him or his family.

I believe that the chief reason that I was selected was the need to get someone who could begin the interviews without months of study. I had spent six years working in files of the Department of Army, the Joint Chiefs of Staff files, the SHAEF files, and Eisenhower's personal papers. I had interviewed nearly all of the British and American Chiefs of Staff except Marshall plus General de Gaulle, and Marshals Juin and de Lattre. I was told that I was the first and only person interviewed for the job. I insisted that I be named the biographer. Since Marshall did not want anything published before his death, they had not stressed the biography in their approach to me but spoke instead of interviews with Marshall and others and the collection and organization of his papers. But they added the biography to the project and I began working toward that end.

LOUIS R. HARLAN, biographer of Booker T. Washington and editor of the Booker T. Washington Papers, published the first volume of the biography simultaneously with the first two volumes of the papers. He explained in a letter to John Y. Cole, October 25, 1983, that the biography

. . . benefited in interpretation and general tone from its long contact with editing. In Washington's case it cannot be said that to comprehend all is to pardon all. His "dirty tricks" and his mealy-mouthed moderation in the face of racial injustice do not look any more attractive when thoroughly examined. But my original purpose was to write a much more detached, ironical, satirical biography. Sustained contact with the documents, and their fuller explanation of how Washington's experience dictated the course he took, changed that approach somewhat. A biographer cannot understand his subject if he keeps him forever at arm's length. The editing helped me to understand more and sit in judgement less. Now that it is all done, in spite of all my efforts I missed the quintessence of Booker T. Washington, the wizard of Tuskegee, but I believe that that is because he had no quintessence. His personality disappeared into the roles he played. So I end with a critical portrait of Washington, but I hope one that is more compassionate and understanding of a black leader born in slavery and flourishing during the age of segregation.

ERNEST SAMUELS, biographer of Henry Adams, in a letter to John Y. Cole, December 2, 1983:

I came to the art or craft of biography writing through one of the many back doors, a doctoral dissertation. I sought in effect to test the reliability of Henry Adams' autobiography, *The Education of Henry Adams*. Could it stand up under scholarly cross examination? The inquiry was a challenge to my earlier training as a lawyer for it brought into play the basic rules of evidence. The experience left me with the conviction that the conscientious biographer stands to a degree in an adversary relation to his subject in the hunt for truth. Perhaps it is a cliche to say he should be bound by "the best evidence" rule. It may not be the way to popular biography but it may bring one closer to the truth. That first volume of mine might have been called "The Education of Henry Adams on Trial."

NOTES ON CONTRIBUTORS

Historian Daniel J. Boorstin has been Librarian of Congress since 1975. The third volume of *The Americans* (New York: Random House, 1973), his most extensive work, won the Pulitzer Prize in 1974. His most recent book is *The Discoverers* (New York: Random House, 1983).

Samuel S. Vaughan, senior vice president and editor of the adult trade division of Random House, was formerly editor-in-chief of Doubleday. He is the author of several children's books and has lectured on publishing at various colleges and universities, including Columbia University, where for five years he taught a course on "The Author and the Publisher."

Edmund Morris's *The Rise of Theodore Roosevelt* (New York: Coward, McCann & Geoghegan, Inc., 1979) won both the Pulitzer Prize and the American Book Award for Biography in 1980, and he is currently completing a second volume. In 1985 he was designated President Ronald Reagan's official biographer.

Historian James Thomas Flexner won the 1973 National Book Award and a special Pulitzer Prize citation for his four-volume biographical study of George Washington published between 1965 and 1972. His one-volume biography *Washington: The Indispensable Man* (Little, Brown) was published in 1974.

David McCullough's books include *Mornings on Horseback* (New York: Simon and Schuster, 1981), the early life of Theodore Roosevelt, which won the 1982 American Book Award for Biography, and *The Path between the Seas: The Creation of the Panama Canal, 1870–1914* (New York: Simon and Schuster, 1977), which won the 1978 National Book Award for History. He is a senior contributing editor of *American Heritage* magazine and the host of the PBS television series "Smithsonian World."

SYMPOSIUM PARTICIPANTS

Paul Nagel *Descent from Glory: Four Generations of the John Adams Family* (1983)
George H. Nash *The Life of Herbert Hoover* (1983)
Forrest Pogue *George C. Marshall* (1963)
Ernest Samuels *The Early Career of Henry Adams* (1973), *Bernard Berensen* (1979)
Samuel S. Schoenbaum *William Shakespeare* (1977)
Jean Strouse *Alice James: A Biography* (1980)
Robert C. Tucker *Stalin as Revolutionary, 1879–1929 (1973)*
Reed Whittemore *William Carlos Williams: Poet from New Jersey* (1975)
Calhoun Winton *Sir Richard Steele, M.P.* (1970)
Jonathan Yardley *Ring: A Biography of Ring Lardner* (1977)

OTHERS

Marie Arana-Ward, senior editor, Harcourt Brace Jovanovich
Robert Aselson, International Thomson, Inc.
Mary Bellor, manager/corporate affairs, Washington Post Co.
Helen Bergan, head, Biography Division, Martin Luther King Library
Simon Michael Bessie, director, Harper & Row Publishers, and chair, National Advisory Board, Center for the Book
Jack Blessington, CBS Television
Daniel J. Boorstin, The Librarian of Congress
Barry Bostwick, actor
John C. Broderick, Assistant Librarian for Research Services, Library of Congress
Joanne Brokaw, CBS Reading Programs
Guy Brown, U.S. Information Agency
W. Michael Brown, executive vice president and chief operating officer, International Thomson Holdings
Ann Carroll, Office of Telecommunications, Smithsonian Institution
Mark Carroll, chief, Professional Publications, U.S. Park Service
Marcus Cohn, Cohn and Marks
John Y. Cole, executive director, Center for the Book
Thomas B. Congdon, president, Congdon and Weed, Inc.
Otto Feurbringer, editor and publishing consultant
Richard Fielder, producer/writer, "George Washington" miniseries
Anne Freedgood, editor, Random House
Ray Fry, U.S. Department of Education

David Fuchs, senior vice president, Broadcast Affairs, and assistant
to the president, CBS/Broadcast Group
Erwin Glikes, president, The Free Press, Macmillan, Inc.
Lynne Grasz, director of communications, CBS/Broadcast Group
Adele Hast, editor-in-chief, Marquis Who's Who, Inc.
Amy Henderson, National Portrait Gallery, Smithsonian Institution
Caroline Hightower, American Institute of Graphic Arts
Joyce Johnson, executive editor, Dial Press
Thomas S. W. Lewis, professor of English, Skidmore College
Gene Mater, senior vice president, Communications and News
Practices, CBS News
Sophie McConnell, American Institute of Graphic Arts
Kenneth McCormick, Doubleday and Company
Frances McCullough, senior editor, Dial Press
George McGhee, Washington, D.C.
Emily McKeigue, editor, G. K. Hall Co.
Maurice Mitchell, Annenberg School of Communications
Judith Chayes Neiman, editor, *Humanities*
Carol Nemeyer, Associate Librarian for National Programs, Library
of Congress
Marc Pachter, assistant director, National Portrait Gallery
Darby Perry, vice president, Franklin Library
Kenneth Petchenik, president, Marquis Who's Who, Inc.
Jean Quinnette, Office of Telecommunications, Smithsonian Insti-
tution
Victoria Robinson, Department of English, Howard University
Richard C. Rowson, director, Duke University Press
Al Silverman, president, Book-of-the-Month Club, Inc.
Samuel S. Vaughan, Doubleday & Co.
Tom Wallace, editor, W. W. Norton & Co.
Michael Weber, Department of History, Carnegie-Mellon University
Betty Wooldridge, director, Blue Ridge Regional Library

THE ART AND PRACTICE OF BIOGRAPHY
A Reading List

The Art of Biography, by Paul Murray Kendall (New York: W.
W. Norton & Co., 1965), reissued with a new prologue by
Stephen B. Oates in 1985
   "Biography hopes to fasten illusion upon reality, to elicit,
   from the coolness of paper, the warmth of a life being
   lived," concludes the biographer of Louis XI and Richard
   III in this succinct volume. In addition to addressing
   the obligations of the contemporary biographer, Kendall
   describes biography in antiquity and in the fifteenth
   century and comments on the history of English biog-
   raphy.
The Biographer's Gift: Life Histories and Humanism, edited by
   James F. Veninga (College Station, Texas: Published for
   the Texas Committee for the Humanities by Texas A & M
   Press, 1983)
   This volume includes three essays: "Biography as an
   Agent of Humanism," by Frank E. Vandiver; "The
   Humanities, the Professions, and the Uses of Biography,"
   by Steven Weiland; and "Biography: The Self and the
   Sacred Canopy," by James F. Veninga. Contributions
   from biographers Robert H. Abzug (Theodore Dwight
   Weld), Stephen B. Oates (John Brown, Nat Turner,
   Abraham Lincoln, Martin Luther King), Ronald Steel
   (Walter Lippman), and Jean Strouse (Alice James)
   demonstrate the craft. The book is based on a program
   sponsored by the Texas Committee for the Humanities
   in 1982.
"The Biographical Novel," by Irving Stone, in *Literary Lectures
Presented at the Library of Congress* (Washington: Library of
Congress, 1973)
   In a lecture presented on January 7, 1957, Stone draws

on his own experience in writing novels based on the lives of Vincent van Gogh, Jessie Fremont, Rachel Jackson, and Mary Todd Lincoln to lay down "a few ground rules" for the practitioner. He also distinguishes between the biographical novel and the fictional novel, the historical novel, or the straight biography and defends the biographical novel against its critics, urging them to judge each succeeding biographical novel on the basis of its writing, research, storytelling, and perception. His own works, he notes, have had two motivations: "I have hoped to feel deeply about simple things; and I have wanted to tell the story of man, against obstacles, for man."

Biography: Fiction, Fact, and Form, by Ira Bruce Nadel (New York: St. Martin's Press, 1984)

Language, structure, and theme in biography are examined by Nadel "to show how in biography language alters fact and draws on fiction to clarify its form." His goal is to demonstrate that biography is "a complex narrative as well as a record of an individual's life, a literary process as well as a historical product." The discussion includes chapters on the "institutionalization" of biography in the nineteenth century and the appearance of the professional biographer.

"Biography, History, and the Writing of Books," by Catherine Drinker Bowen, in *The Art of History* (Washington: Library of Congress, 1967)

A 1967 lecture presented at the Library of Congress in which the author, a biographer of John Adams and Oliver Wendell Holmes, discusses her work. She is fortunate to be a biographer, she feels, because "history and biography, outside the schools, are neither enslaved nor betrayed by fashions in form or philosophy." It is the business of the biographer "to tell his story as clearly, as authentically, and as entertainingly as he can."

"Confessions of a Biographer," by Ernest Samuels, *Quarterly Journal of the Library of Congress* 38 (Winter 1981): 34–41

A self-styled "scholar turned biographer" who has "a

strong prejudice in favor of reliable evidence and scholarly objectivity," Samuels explains how he chose his two biographical subjects, Henry Adams and Bernard Berenson, and describes the research behind his books.

Golden Codgers: Biographical Speculations, by Richard Ellman (New York: Oxford University Press, 1973)

Nine essays by the biographer of James Joyce and William Butler Yeats. The first, "Literary Biography," was a lecture delivered at Oxford University in 1971. Other essays emphasize individual writers, particularly George Eliot, Oscar Wilde, André Gide, Arthur Symmons, and T. S. Eliot.

Humanities, June 1984

An issue of the National Endowment for the Humanities' bimonthly review that focuses on biography. The contents include "Lifeline: The Evolution of Biography," by historian Marc Pachter; "Lives That Matter," by publisher Thomas Congdon; an interview with Forrest C. Pogue, biographer of Gen. George C. Marshall; "Why History Scorns Biography," by historian John A. Garraty, editor of the *Dictionary of American Biography*; and "The Return of Marcus Garvey," by historian Robert A. Hill.

"Literary Biography" by Joseph Epstein. *New Criterion* 1 (May 1983): 27–37

"The one indisputable point about modern literary biographies is their propensity to grow longer and longer," notes critic Epstein in this informative essay on the changing nature of biographical writing.

The Nature of Biography, by Robert Gittings (Seattle: University of Washington Press, 1978)

Three lectures presented in 1977 by the biographer of John Keats and Thomas Hardy at the University of Washington under the title "The Art and Science of Biography." The lectures, "Past History," "Present Practice," and "Paths of Progress," were planned as a "comprehensive view of biographical writing by English writers on English subjects."

New Directions in Biography, edited and with a foreword by

Anthony M. Friedson (Honolulu: Published for the Biographical Research Center by the University of Hawaii, 1981)

The proceedings of an international symposium on biography sponsored by the Biographical Research Center of the University of Hawaii. The papers include "Biography and the Science of Man," by Leon Edel, "Literary and Historical Biography," by Michael Holroyd, "Group Biography," by Margot Peters, and considerations of biography in South Africa, France, and Japan.

"Phyllis Grosskurth's Interviews with Literary Biographers: I. George Painter, II. Robert Gittings," *Salmagundi*, no. 61 (Fall 1983): 22–50

Phyllis Grosskurth, biographer of Havelock Ellis, quizzes biographers George Painter (who wrote about Caxton, Gide, Proust, and Chateaubriand) and Robert Gittings (biographer of Keats and Hardy) about the nature of biography, how they chose their subjects, and their writing (and reading) habits. The interviews were conducted in 1980–81.

Telling Lives: The Biographer's Art, edited by Marc Pachter (Philadelphia: University of Pennsylvania Press, 1981)

Essays about biography by historian Marc Pachter, biographers Leon Edel (Henry James), Justin Kaplan (Mark Twain, Walt Whitman), Doris Kearns (Lyndon B. Johnson), Theodore Rosengarten (Nate Shaw), and Geoffrey Wolff (Harry Crosby), historian Barbara Tuchman, and critic Alfred Kazin. The book grew out of a symposium on "The Art of Biography" at the National Portrait Gallery, Smithsonian Institution.

Writing Lives: Principia Biographica, by Leon Edel (New York: Norton, 1984)

A "summing up" of his lifework by the biographer best known for his books about Henry James and about the Bloomsbury Group. An updating of Edel's *Literary Biography* (1957) to which he has added papers about what he calls the New Biography.

Yale Review 73 (Autumn 1983 and Winter 1984)
Two special issues devoted to "The Telling of Lives,"
the "uses of biography and autobiography in fiction,
poetry, history, literary criticism, and ethnography."
Contributors include Daniel Aaron, Robert Coles, Erik
H. Erikson, John Hersey, R. W. B. Lewis, Jonathan
Spence, and C. Vann Woodward.

◫

Biography & Books, *edited by John Y. Cole, has been printed in an edition of 1,500 copies. The typeface for the cover and text is Mergenthaler's Linotron Baskerville No. 2, set by Monotype Composition Company, Baltimore, Maryland.*

The text stock is Mohawk Superfine, an acid-free paper manufactured in Cohoes, New York, and the cover is Simpson Filare, supplied by Simpson Paper Company, San Francisco, California. Zanders Feinpapiere AG in West Germany manufactured the Ikonofix Matte Dull 42 Mauve that was inserted between the cover and text.

Biography & Books *was printed at Garamond/Pridemark Press, Inc., Baltimore, Maryland, by offset lithography and assembled in Columbia, Maryland, at American Trade Bindery.*

Designed by James E. Conner.